Table of Contents

- Chapter 1: Introduction to Multimodal AI 3
  - What is Multimodal AI? 3
  - Advantages of Multimodal AI 4
  - Applications of Multimodal AI 5
  - Overview of the Book 6
- Chapter 2: Multimodal AI in Healthcare 7
  - Diagnosis and Treatment Planning 7
  - Medical Imaging Analysis 8
  - Patient Data Analysis 9
- Chapter 3: Multimodal AI in Autonomous Vehicles 11
  - Data Processing for Navigation 11
  - Real-time Decision Making 12
  - Sensor Integration 13
- Chapter 4: Multimodal AI in Customer Service 14
  - Personalized Responses 14
  - Empathetic Interactions 15
  - Text, Voice, and Facial Analysis 16
- Chapter 5: Multimodal AI in Education 18
  - Adaptive Learning Styles 18
  - Interactive Lessons and Assessments 19
  - Incorporating Text, Images, and Audio 20
- Chapter 6: Multimodal AI in Media and Entertainment 21
  - Personalized Recommendations 21
  - Content Generation 22
  - User Preferences Analysis 23
- Chapter 7: Multimodal AI in Cybersecurity 24
  - Threat Detection and Response 25
  - Text and Network Traffic Analysis 25
  - System Log Analysis 26

Chapter 8: Multimodal AI in Smart Homes 27
- Voice Command Integration 27
- Sensor Data Automation 29
- Home Task Enhancement 30

Chapter 9: Multimodal AI in Finance 31
- Investment Decision Making 31
- News and Market Data Analysis 32
- Financial Report Analysis 33

Chapter 10: Multimodal AI in Social Media 34
- Trend Detection 34
- Sentiment Analysis 35
- Fake News Detection 36

Chapter 11: Multimodal AI in Language Translation 38
- Real-time Translation 38
- Communication Facilitation 39
- Text, Speech, and Image Translation 40

Chapter 12: Conclusion 41
- Summary of Key Points 41
- Future Trends in Multimodal AI 41
- Recommendations for Professionals 43

Chapter 1: Introduction to Multimodal AI

What is Multimodal AI?

Multimodal AI refers to artificial intelligence systems that are capable of processing and generating multiple types of data, such as text, images, audio, and more. This technology has revolutionized the capabilities of AI applications, enabling the development of more sophisticated virtual assistants and interactive systems that can understand and respond in more human-like ways. By incorporating multiple modalities of data, these systems are able to provide more comprehensive and nuanced responses, enhancing the overall user experience.

One of the key areas where multimodal AI is making a significant impact is in the field of healthcare. AI systems can now analyze medical images, text reports, and patient data to assist in diagnosis and treatment planning. By combining multiple types of data, these systems are able to provide more accurate and personalized insights, ultimately improving patient outcomes and reducing healthcare costs.

In the realm of autonomous vehicles, multimodal AI is playing a crucial role in enabling these vehicles to navigate and make decisions in real-time. By processing data from cameras, lidar, radar, and sensors, AI systems can effectively interpret their surroundings and respond accordingly, ensuring safe and efficient transportation. This technology is paving the way for the widespread adoption of autonomous vehicles and revolutionizing the future of transportation.

Multimodal AI is also being utilized in customer service applications, where AI systems can analyze text, voice, and facial expressions to provide personalized and empathetic responses to customers. By incorporating multiple modalities of data, these systems are able to better understand and address customer needs, ultimately enhancing customer satisfaction and loyalty. This technology is transforming the way businesses interact with their customers and improving overall customer experiences.

In conclusion, multimodal AI is a groundbreaking technology that is revolutionizing a wide range of industries, from healthcare to finance to education. By leveraging multiple types of data, AI systems are able to provide more comprehensive and nuanced insights, ultimately improving decision-making processes and enhancing user experiences. As this technology continues to evolve and advance, we can expect to see even greater innovations and advancements in the field of artificial intelligence.

Advantages of Multimodal AI

Multimodal AI, which refers to AI systems that can process and generate multiple types of data such as text, images, and audio, offers a multitude of advantages in various industries and applications. One key advantage of multimodal AI is its ability to improve the capabilities of AI applications, enabling more sophisticated virtual assistants and interactive AI systems that can understand and respond in more human-like ways. This has led to a significant enhancement in user experience and engagement, making AI systems more intuitive and user-friendly.

In the healthcare industry, multimodal AI has proven to be invaluable in assisting with diagnosis and treatment planning. AI systems that can analyze medical images, text reports, and patient data are able to provide healthcare professionals with more accurate and timely information, leading to better patient outcomes. This technology has the potential to revolutionize the way medical professionals work, saving time and improving overall efficiency in healthcare settings.

Another key area where multimodal AI shines is in autonomous vehicles. AI systems that can process data from cameras, lidar, radar, and sensors are essential for navigating and making real-time decisions on the road. These systems have the potential to significantly improve road safety, reduce accidents, and pave the way for the widespread adoption of autonomous vehicles in the future.

Multimodal AI also plays a crucial role in customer service, education, media and entertainment, cybersecurity, smart homes, finance, social media, and language translation. In customer service, AI systems can analyze text, voice, and facial expressions to provide personalized and empathetic responses to customers, enhancing the overall customer experience. In education, AI systems can adapt to different learning styles by incorporating text, images, and audio in interactive lessons and assessments, making learning more engaging and effective.

Overall, the advantages of multimodal AI are vast and far-reaching, impacting a wide range of industries and applications. As this technology continues to advance and evolve, professionals in various fields can expect to see even more innovative and transformative uses of multimodal AI in the future.

Applications of Multimodal AI

Advancements in Multimodal AI have opened up a world of possibilities for professionals across various industries. One of the key applications of Multimodal AI is in the development of more sophisticated virtual assistants and interactive AI systems. These systems are now capable of processing and generating multiple types of data, such as text, images, and audio, allowing them to understand and respond in more human-like ways. This has revolutionized the way we interact with AI technology, making it more intuitive and user-friendly.

In the healthcare industry, Multimodal AI is being used to analyze medical images, text reports, and patient data to assist in diagnosis and treatment planning. This has the potential to improve the accuracy and efficiency of medical care, leading to better patient outcomes. Similarly, in the field of autonomous vehicles, Multimodal AI is playing a crucial role in processing data from cameras, lidar, radar, and sensors to navigate and make decisions in real-time. This technology is paving the way for safer and more efficient transportation systems.

Multimodal AI is also being utilized in customer service to provide personalized and empathetic responses to customers. By analyzing text, voice, and facial expressions, AI systems can better understand customer needs and tailor their interactions accordingly. In the education sector, Multimodal AI is being used to adapt to different learning styles by incorporating text, images, and audio in interactive lessons and assessments. This personalized approach to learning is revolutionizing the way students engage with educational content.

In media and entertainment, Multimodal AI is being used to generate personalized recommendations and content based on user preferences across different types of media. This has transformed the way we consume entertainment, making it more tailored to individual tastes. In cybersecurity, Multimodal AI is playing a crucial role in detecting and responding to threats by analyzing text, network traffic, and system logs. This proactive approach to cybersecurity is essential in protecting sensitive data and preventing potential breaches.

Overall, the applications of Multimodal AI are vast and diverse, spanning across industries such as finance, social media, language translation, and smart homes. As professionals in these fields continue to explore the potential of Multimodal AI, we can expect to see even more innovative solutions that leverage the power of AI systems that can process and generate multiple types of data.

Overview of the Book

The book "Advancements in Multimodal AI: A Guide for Professionals" provides a comprehensive overview of the rapidly evolving field of multimodal artificial intelligence. Multimodal AI refers to AI systems that can process and generate multiple types of data, including text, images, and audio. This book is designed for professionals who are looking to stay ahead of the curve and leverage the latest advancements in AI technology to enhance their work.

One of the key areas covered in the book is the use of multimodal AI in healthcare. AI systems are being developed that can analyze medical images, text reports, and patient data to assist in diagnosis and treatment planning. These systems have the potential to revolutionize the healthcare industry by improving accuracy and efficiency in medical decision-making.

Another important application of multimodal AI explored in the book is in the realm of autonomous vehicles. AI systems are being used to process data from cameras, lidar, radar, and sensors to navigate and make decisions in real-time. This technology is paving the way for safer and more efficient transportation systems.

In addition to healthcare and autonomous vehicles, the book also delves into the use of multimodal AI in customer service, education, media and entertainment, cybersecurity, smart homes, finance, social media, and language translation. Each of these areas presents unique opportunities for professionals to leverage AI technology to enhance their work and deliver more personalized and efficient services.

Overall, "Advancements in Multimodal AI: A Guide for Professionals" serves as a valuable resource for professionals looking to understand and harness the power of multimodal AI in their respective fields. With real-world examples and practical insights, this book provides a roadmap for professionals to navigate the complex landscape of AI technology and drive innovation in their industries.

Chapter 2: Multimodal AI in Healthcare

Diagnosis and Treatment Planning

Diagnosis and Treatment Planning in the field of Multimodal AI is a crucial step in utilizing artificial intelligence to improve healthcare outcomes. By integrating AI systems that can analyze medical images, text reports, and patient data, healthcare professionals can receive more accurate and timely diagnoses, leading to more effective treatment planning. These AI systems can assist in identifying patterns and anomalies in medical data that may not be immediately apparent to human practitioners, ultimately improving the quality of care provided to patients.

In the realm of autonomous vehicles, Multimodal AI plays a key role in enabling these vehicles to navigate and make decisions in real-time. By processing data from cameras, lidar, radar, and sensors, AI systems can help autonomous vehicles safely maneuver through complex environments with precision and efficiency. This technology is essential for the development of self-driving cars and other autonomous vehicles, as it allows them to perceive and respond to their surroundings in a way that mimics human perception.

For professionals working in customer service, Multimodal AI offers the opportunity to provide personalized and empathetic responses to customers. By analyzing text, voice, and facial expressions, AI systems can understand and respond to customer inquiries in a more human-like manner. This capability not only enhances the customer experience but also streamlines customer service operations by automating routine tasks and providing faster, more accurate responses.

In the field of education, Multimodal AI is revolutionizing the way students learn by adapting to different learning styles through interactive lessons and assessments. By incorporating text, images, and audio into educational materials, AI systems can engage students more effectively and provide personalized feedback to help them succeed. This technology has the potential to improve learning outcomes and make education more accessible and engaging for students of all ages.

In conclusion, the advancements in Multimodal AI are transforming various industries by enabling AI systems to process and generate multiple types of data in more sophisticated and human-like ways. From healthcare to autonomous vehicles, customer service to education, Multimodal AI is revolutionizing the way professionals work and interact with technology. By leveraging the capabilities of Multimodal AI, professionals can improve outcomes, enhance experiences, and drive innovation in their respective fields.

Medical Imaging Analysis

Medical imaging analysis is a critical component of healthcare, allowing professionals to diagnose and treat various medical conditions. With the advancements in multimodal AI, medical imaging analysis has become more accurate and efficient than ever before. AI systems can now analyze medical images, text reports, and patient data to assist healthcare professionals in making informed decisions regarding patient care.

One of the key benefits of multimodal AI in medical imaging analysis is the ability to detect subtle abnormalities that may be missed by the human eye. AI systems can analyze images from multiple modalities, such as MRI, CT scans, and X-rays, to provide a comprehensive view of a patient's condition. This can lead to earlier detection of diseases and more personalized treatment plans for patients.

Furthermore, multimodal AI can help healthcare professionals prioritize cases based on the severity of the condition. By analyzing both medical images and patient data, AI systems can identify patterns and correlations that can help determine the urgency of a particular case. This can help streamline the workflow of healthcare professionals and ensure that patients receive timely and appropriate care.

In addition to diagnosis and treatment planning, multimodal AI in medical imaging analysis can also aid in monitoring a patient's progress over time. By analyzing sequential imaging studies and patient data, AI systems can track changes in a patient's condition and provide insights into the effectiveness of treatment. This can help healthcare professionals adjust treatment plans as needed to optimize patient outcomes.

Overall, the integration of multimodal AI in medical imaging analysis has the potential to revolutionize healthcare by providing more accurate, efficient, and personalized care to patients. As AI technologies continue to advance, we can expect to see even greater improvements in medical imaging analysis, leading to better outcomes for patients and healthcare professionals alike.

Patient Data Analysis

In the realm of healthcare, the application of Multimodal AI for patient data analysis has revolutionized the way medical professionals diagnose and treat patients. By utilizing AI systems that can analyze medical images, text reports, and patient data, healthcare providers are able to make more accurate and timely decisions for their patients. This technology has the potential to improve patient outcomes and streamline the healthcare process.

One of the key advantages of using Multimodal AI for patient data analysis is its ability to process and interpret multiple types of data simultaneously. This means that AI systems can take into account a wide range of information, including patient histories, lab results, imaging studies, and more, to provide a comprehensive analysis of a patient's condition. This holistic approach allows healthcare providers to make more informed decisions and tailor treatment plans to individual patients.

Furthermore, Multimodal AI systems can assist healthcare professionals in identifying patterns and trends in patient data that may not be immediately apparent to the human eye. By analyzing large amounts of data quickly and accurately, AI systems can help providers identify potential risks, predict outcomes, and make proactive decisions to improve patient care. This can ultimately lead to better patient outcomes and more efficient healthcare delivery.

In addition to aiding in diagnosis and treatment planning, Multimodal AI for patient data analysis can also help healthcare organizations improve their operational efficiency. By automating tasks such as data entry, documentation, and billing, AI systems can free up healthcare professionals to focus more on patient care. This not only improves the patient experience but also helps healthcare organizations reduce costs and increase productivity.

Overall, the use of Multimodal AI for patient data analysis holds great promise for the future of healthcare. By harnessing the power of AI to analyze and interpret complex patient data, healthcare providers can improve diagnostic accuracy, optimize treatment plans, and enhance the overall quality of care for patients. As this technology continues to evolve, we can expect to see even greater advancements in patient care and healthcare delivery.

Chapter 3: Multimodal AI in Autonomous Vehicles

Data Processing for Navigation

Data processing for navigation is a crucial aspect of developing multimodal AI systems that can effectively navigate and make decisions in real-time. Whether it's for autonomous vehicles, virtual assistants, or smart home devices, the ability to process data from various sources such as cameras, lidar, radar, sensors, and more is essential for ensuring safe and efficient navigation.

In the realm of autonomous vehicles, data processing for navigation involves analyzing and interpreting data from multiple sensors to make decisions about speed, direction, and potential obstacles on the road. This requires sophisticated algorithms that can process large amounts of data quickly and accurately to ensure the vehicle can navigate complex environments with precision.

For virtual assistants and interactive AI systems, data processing for navigation involves understanding and responding to user commands in a human-like manner. By analyzing text, voice, and even facial expressions, these systems can provide personalized and empathetic responses that enhance the user experience and make interactions more natural and intuitive.

In the healthcare industry, data processing for navigation plays a critical role in assisting with diagnosis and treatment planning. AI systems that can analyze medical images, text reports, and patient data can help healthcare professionals make more informed decisions and provide better care to patients.

Overall, data processing for navigation is a fundamental aspect of developing advanced multimodal AI systems across various industries. By harnessing the power of AI to analyze and interpret data from multiple sources, professionals can create more sophisticated and efficient solutions that improve safety, efficiency, and user experience in a wide range of applications.

Real-time Decision Making

Real-time decision making is a crucial aspect of Multimodal AI systems, as they are designed to process and generate multiple types of data simultaneously. These systems have the ability to analyze various forms of data, such as text, images, audio, and more, in real-time, allowing for faster and more accurate decision-making processes. This capability is especially important in applications where quick responses are necessary, such as autonomous vehicles, healthcare, customer service, and cybersecurity.

In the realm of autonomous vehicles, Multimodal AI systems play a vital role in navigating and making decisions in real-time. These systems can process data from cameras, lidar, radar, and sensors to quickly assess their surroundings and make split-second decisions to avoid obstacles and ensure safe navigation. Real-time decision making is essential in this context, as any delay could result in potential accidents or safety hazards.

Similarly, in healthcare, Multimodal AI systems are used to assist in diagnosis and treatment planning by analyzing medical images, text reports, and patient data. The ability to make real-time decisions based on this multimodal data is crucial for healthcare professionals to provide accurate and timely care to patients. By leveraging the power of Multimodal AI, healthcare providers can improve patient outcomes and streamline their workflow.

In customer service, Multimodal AI systems are employed to analyze text, voice, and facial expressions to provide personalized and empathetic responses to customers. Real-time decision making is essential in this context to ensure that customer queries are addressed promptly and effectively. By incorporating multiple modalities of data, these systems can better understand customer needs and provide tailored solutions in real-time, ultimately enhancing the overall customer experience.

Overall, real-time decision making is a fundamental aspect of Multimodal AI systems across various industries, from healthcare to autonomous vehicles to customer service. By harnessing the power of multiple types of data and making quick and accurate decisions in real-time, these systems are revolutionizing the way professionals work and interact with AI technology.

Sensor Integration

Sensor integration is a crucial aspect of developing advanced multimodal AI systems. In order to process and generate multiple types of data, such as text, images, audio, and sensor data, these systems must seamlessly integrate information from various sources. By incorporating data from sensors into the AI algorithms, these systems can make more informed decisions and provide more accurate responses in real-time.

In the realm of autonomous vehicles, sensor integration plays a vital role in enabling AI systems to navigate and make split-second decisions. Cameras, lidar, radar, and other sensors provide valuable data that allows these vehicles to detect obstacles, anticipate changes in traffic patterns, and respond to road conditions. By integrating data from multiple sensors, autonomous vehicles can operate safely and efficiently in complex environments.

In the healthcare industry, sensor integration is revolutionizing the way medical professionals diagnose and treat patients. AI systems that can analyze medical images, text reports, and patient data are able to provide more accurate and personalized recommendations for treatment. By integrating sensor data into these systems, healthcare providers can improve patient outcomes and streamline the diagnostic process.

In the field of customer service, sensor integration enables AI systems to provide more personalized and empathetic responses to customers. By analyzing text, voice, and facial expressions, these systems can better understand customer needs and preferences. Sensor integration allows AI systems to adapt and respond in real-time, creating a more seamless and interactive experience for users.

Overall, sensor integration is a critical component of advancing multimodal AI systems across various industries. By incorporating data from sensors into AI algorithms, these systems can process and generate multiple types of data more effectively, leading to more sophisticated and human-like interactions. As technology continues to evolve, sensor integration will play a key role in shaping the future of AI applications.

Chapter 4: Multimodal AI in Customer Service

Personalized Responses

In the world of Multimodal AI, personalized responses are becoming increasingly important as AI systems are expected to interact with users in a more human-like manner. These personalized responses are tailored to the individual user's preferences, needs, and emotions, making the interaction more engaging and effective. Whether it's a virtual assistant providing assistance with daily tasks, a healthcare AI system helping with diagnosis and treatment planning, or an autonomous vehicle making split-second decisions, personalized responses play a crucial role in enhancing the user experience.

One of the key applications of personalized responses in Multimodal AI is in customer service. AI systems are now able to analyze text, voice, and facial expressions to provide personalized and empathetic responses to customers. This not only improves customer satisfaction but also helps businesses better understand their customers' needs and preferences. By utilizing personalized responses, AI systems can build stronger relationships with customers, leading to increased loyalty and trust.

In the field of education, personalized responses are revolutionizing the way students learn and interact with AI systems. By incorporating text, images, and audio in interactive lessons and assessments, AI systems can adapt to different learning styles and provide tailored feedback to students. This personalized approach not only improves learning outcomes but also helps students stay engaged and motivated. Educators are now able to leverage AI technology to create more dynamic and personalized learning experiences for their students.

In the realm of media and entertainment, personalized responses are driving the development of AI systems that can generate personalized recommendations and content based on user preferences. Whether it's recommending a movie, a song, or a news article, AI systems are now able to analyze user behavior and preferences across different types of media to provide a customized experience. This level of personalization not only enhances user satisfaction but also helps businesses better target their audience and increase engagement.

Overall, personalized responses are shaping the future of Multimodal AI by enabling AI systems to interact with users in more meaningful and personalized ways. From customer service to education to media and entertainment, personalized responses are transforming the user experience and opening up new possibilities for AI applications. As AI technology continues to advance, the importance of personalized responses will only grow, leading to more sophisticated and human-like interactions between AI systems and users.

Empathetic Interactions

In the realm of artificial intelligence, the concept of empathetic interactions is gaining traction as AI systems become more sophisticated and human-like. Empathy is the ability to understand and share the feelings of others, and incorporating this trait into AI systems can greatly enhance the user experience. Whether it's in virtual assistants, healthcare, autonomous vehicles, customer service, education, media and entertainment, cybersecurity, smart homes, finance, social media, or language translation, the potential for empathetic interactions is vast.

One of the key benefits of empathetic interactions in AI is the ability to provide personalized and tailored responses to users. By analyzing data from various sources such as text, voice, and facial expressions, AI systems can understand the emotional state of the user and respond in a way that is empathetic and supportive. This can be especially important in healthcare, where patients may be dealing with sensitive issues and need compassionate care and understanding from AI systems.

In customer service, the ability to provide empathetic responses can greatly enhance the customer experience and build trust and loyalty. By analyzing text, voice, and facial expressions, AI systems can detect the emotions of customers and respond in a way that shows empathy and understanding. This can lead to more satisfied customers and increased loyalty to the brand.

In education, empathetic interactions can help to create a more engaging and personalized learning experience for students. By incorporating text, images, and audio in interactive lessons and assessments, AI systems can adapt to different learning styles and provide feedback that is tailored to the individual student. This can help to improve student engagement and retention, leading to better learning outcomes.

Overall, the incorporation of empathetic interactions in AI systems has the potential to revolutionize the way we interact with technology. By understanding and responding to the emotions of users, AI systems can create more human-like interactions that are more engaging, supportive, and empathetic. This can lead to improved user experiences in a wide range of industries and applications, making AI systems more valuable and effective tools for professionals.

Text, Voice, and Facial Analysis

In the realm of AI technology, advancements in multimodal AI have opened up new possibilities for professionals across various industries. Multimodal AI systems are capable of processing and generating multiple types of data, including text, images, audio, and more. This has paved the way for more sophisticated virtual assistants and interactive AI systems that can understand and respond in more human-like ways. By combining different modalities of data, multimodal AI has the potential to revolutionize the way we interact with technology.

One key application of multimodal AI is in the field of healthcare, where AI systems can analyze medical images, text reports, and patient data to assist in diagnosis and treatment planning. By leveraging multiple types of data, healthcare professionals can make more informed decisions and provide better care for their patients. Additionally, multimodal AI has the potential to improve efficiency and accuracy in healthcare settings, ultimately leading to better patient outcomes.

Another area where multimodal AI is making a significant impact is in autonomous vehicles. AI systems that can process data from cameras, lidar, radar, and sensors to navigate and make decisions in real-time are essential for the development of self-driving cars. By combining different modalities of data, autonomous vehicles can better understand their surroundings and react to changing conditions, making transportation safer and more efficient.

In the realm of customer service, multimodal AI systems are being used to analyze text, voice, and facial expressions to provide personalized and empathetic responses to customers. By incorporating multiple modalities of data, AI systems can better understand customer needs and preferences, leading to more satisfying interactions. This can result in improved customer satisfaction and loyalty, ultimately benefiting businesses and consumers alike.

Overall, the integration of text, voice, and facial analysis in multimodal AI systems holds great promise for professionals in a wide range of industries. Whether it be in healthcare, autonomous vehicles, customer service, education, media and entertainment, cybersecurity, smart homes, finance, social media, or language translation, the possibilities for leveraging multimodal AI are endless. As professionals continue to explore and develop these technologies, the potential for innovation and advancement in AI will only continue to grow.

Chapter 5: Multimodal AI in Education

Adaptive Learning Styles

Adaptive learning styles are a crucial aspect of multimodal AI systems, as they allow for personalized and tailored educational experiences for users. With the ability to incorporate text, images, and audio in interactive lessons and assessments, AI systems can adapt to different learning preferences and styles. This means that individuals who learn best through visual aids can benefit from image-based lessons, while auditory learners can engage with audio-based content. By catering to diverse learning styles, AI systems can enhance the overall effectiveness of educational experiences and improve the retention of information.

In the realm of healthcare, adaptive learning styles play a vital role in assisting with diagnosis and treatment planning. Multimodal AI systems can analyze medical images, text reports, and patient data to provide healthcare professionals with comprehensive and personalized insights. By adapting to the specific needs of each patient, AI systems can help streamline decision-making processes and improve the overall quality of care. This level of customization and personalization is essential in the healthcare industry, where individualized treatment plans can have a significant impact on patient outcomes.

In the field of autonomous vehicles, adaptive learning styles are essential for enabling real-time navigation and decision-making capabilities. Multimodal AI systems can process data from cameras, lidar, radar, and sensors to navigate complex environments and make split-second decisions. By adapting to changing road conditions and traffic patterns, AI systems can enhance the safety and efficiency of autonomous vehicles. This level of adaptability is crucial for ensuring the reliability and effectiveness of self-driving technologies in a variety of real-world scenarios.

In customer service applications, adaptive learning styles are key to providing personalized and empathetic responses to customers. Multimodal AI systems can analyze text, voice, and facial expressions to understand and respond to customer inquiries in a human-like manner. By adapting to the emotional cues and preferences of each customer, AI systems can enhance the overall customer experience and build stronger relationships. This level of personalization is essential for improving customer satisfaction and loyalty in a competitive market.

In conclusion, adaptive learning styles are a fundamental component of multimodal AI systems across a variety of industries and applications. By incorporating text, images, and audio in interactive experiences, AI systems can adapt to different preferences and styles to provide personalized and tailored solutions. Whether in education, healthcare, autonomous vehicles, or customer service, adaptive learning styles play a crucial role in enhancing the effectiveness and efficiency of AI technologies. As the capabilities of multimodal AI continue to advance, the importance of adaptive learning styles will only grow in significance for professionals in the field.

Interactive Lessons and Assessments

Interactive lessons and assessments are crucial components of the educational process, and with the advancements in multimodal AI, these traditional methods are being revolutionized. In the field of education, AI systems are now able to adapt to different learning styles by incorporating various types of data such as text, images, and audio in interactive lessons and assessments. This allows for a more personalized and effective learning experience for students, as the AI systems can tailor the content to meet the specific needs and preferences of each individual learner.

One of the key benefits of using multimodal AI in interactive lessons and assessments is the ability to provide real-time feedback to students. With AI systems that can analyze and understand different types of data, teachers can quickly assess student performance and provide feedback that is tailored to each student's individual needs. This not only helps students to improve their understanding of the material, but also allows teachers to identify areas where additional support may be needed.

Furthermore, the use of multimodal AI in interactive lessons and assessments can help to increase student engagement and motivation. By incorporating various types of data into the learning process, students are more likely to stay engaged and interested in the material. This can lead to improved learning outcomes and a more positive overall learning experience for students.

In addition to enhancing the learning experience for students, multimodal AI in interactive lessons and assessments can also benefit teachers. By automating certain aspects of the assessment process and providing real-time feedback, teachers can save time and resources that can be better spent on other aspects of their teaching responsibilities. This can lead to a more efficient and effective teaching environment, ultimately benefiting both teachers and students.

Overall, the use of multimodal AI in interactive lessons and assessments represents a significant advancement in the field of education. By incorporating various types of data into the learning process, AI systems can provide a more personalized, engaging, and effective learning experience for students, while also benefiting teachers by automating certain aspects of the assessment process. As AI technology continues to evolve, the possibilities for enhancing the educational experience through multimodal AI are endless.

Incorporating Text, Images, and Audio

In the world of artificial intelligence, the ability to process and generate multiple types of data - such as text, images, and audio - is becoming increasingly important. This capability, known as multimodal AI, is revolutionizing the way AI systems interact with and understand the world around them. By incorporating multiple types of data, AI systems are able to provide more personalized and human-like responses, making them invaluable tools in a variety of industries.

One area where multimodal AI is making a significant impact is in healthcare. AI systems that can analyze medical images, text reports, and patient data are helping doctors to diagnose illnesses more accurately and develop personalized treatment plans. This not only improves patient outcomes but also helps to reduce healthcare costs by streamlining the diagnostic process.

Autonomous vehicles are another area where multimodal AI is proving to be indispensable. By processing data from cameras, lidar, radar, and sensors, AI systems are able to navigate complex environments and make split-second decisions in real-time. This technology is not only making our roads safer but also paving the way for a future where self-driving cars are the norm.

In the realm of customer service, multimodal AI is transforming the way companies interact with their customers. By analyzing text, voice, and facial expressions, AI systems are able to provide personalized and empathetic responses to customer inquiries. This not only improves customer satisfaction but also helps companies to better understand their customers' needs and preferences.

Education is another area where multimodal AI is having a profound impact. By incorporating text, images, and audio in interactive lessons and assessments, AI systems are able to adapt to different learning styles and provide personalized feedback to students. This not only enhances the learning experience but also helps educators to identify areas where individual students may need additional support.

Overall, the integration of text, images, and audio in AI systems is opening up a world of possibilities across a wide range of industries. From healthcare to autonomous vehicles, customer service to education, the applications of multimodal AI are vast and varied. As technology continues to advance, we can expect to see even greater innovations in the field of multimodal AI, shaping the way we interact with and understand the world around us.

Chapter 6: Multimodal AI in Media and Entertainment

Personalized Recommendations

Personalized recommendations are a key feature of many AI systems, including those utilizing multimodal capabilities. These recommendations are tailored to individual users based on their preferences, behavior, and past interactions with the system. By leveraging data from multiple sources such as text, images, and audio, AI can provide more accurate and relevant suggestions to users across various industries.

In the realm of healthcare, personalized recommendations can help medical professionals make more informed decisions when diagnosing and treating patients. By analyzing medical images, text reports, and patient data, AI systems can recommend the most effective treatment options based on individual characteristics and medical history. This not only improves patient outcomes but also enhances the efficiency of healthcare providers.

For autonomous vehicles, personalized recommendations play a crucial role in ensuring safe and efficient navigation. By processing data from cameras, lidar, radar, and sensors, AI systems can make real-time decisions that are tailored to the specific driving conditions and preferences of the user. This level of personalization is essential for enhancing the overall driving experience and reducing the risk of accidents.

In the customer service industry, personalized recommendations enable AI systems to provide more empathetic and effective responses to users. By analyzing text, voice, and facial expressions, these systems can better understand the needs and emotions of customers, leading to more satisfying interactions. This personalized approach not only improves customer satisfaction but also builds brand loyalty and trust.

In the realm of media and entertainment, personalized recommendations are transforming the way content is consumed. By analyzing user preferences across different types of media, AI systems can generate recommendations that are tailored to individual tastes and interests. This not only enhances the user experience but also helps content creators and distributors better understand their audience and deliver more engaging and relevant content.

Content Generation

Content generation is a crucial aspect of advancing multimodal AI technology. With the ability to process and generate multiple types of data such as text, images, audio, and more, AI systems are becoming increasingly sophisticated. This expansion of capabilities has allowed for the development of more human-like virtual assistants and interactive AI systems that can understand and respond to users in more natural ways.

In the realm of healthcare, multimodal AI systems are revolutionizing the way medical imaging is analyzed and patient data is processed. By combining text reports, medical images, and patient information, these AI systems are able to assist healthcare professionals in diagnosis and treatment planning, ultimately leading to more accurate and efficient care for patients.

Autonomous vehicles are another area where multimodal AI is making significant advancements. AI systems that can process data from cameras, lidar, radar, and sensors are enabling vehicles to navigate and make decisions in real-time. This technology is critical for the development of safe and efficient autonomous vehicles that can operate without human intervention.

In customer service, multimodal AI systems are being used to provide personalized and empathetic responses to customers. By analyzing text, voice, and facial expressions, these AI systems can tailor their interactions to meet the individual needs of each customer, creating a more positive and engaging customer service experience.

In education, multimodal AI systems are transforming the way students learn by incorporating text, images, and audio in interactive lessons and assessments. By adapting to different learning styles, these AI systems are able to provide a more personalized and effective learning experience for students, ultimately leading to improved educational outcomes.

User Preferences Analysis

Understanding user preferences is crucial for the success of any AI system, especially in the realm of multimodal AI. By analyzing user behavior and feedback, developers can tailor the system to better meet the needs and expectations of the users. This can lead to higher user satisfaction, increased engagement, and ultimately, better performance of the AI system.

In the context of multimodal AI for healthcare, user preferences analysis can help in designing systems that are intuitive and easy to use for medical professionals. By understanding how doctors and nurses interact with the system, developers can optimize the interface and functionalities to streamline the diagnosis and treatment process. Additionally, analyzing patient preferences can lead to more personalized and effective healthcare recommendations and interventions.

In the field of autonomous vehicles, user preferences analysis is essential for ensuring the safety and comfort of passengers. By studying how users interact with the vehicle's interface and respond to different stimuli, developers can design systems that provide a smooth and enjoyable driving experience. Understanding user preferences can also help in improving decision-making algorithms to better anticipate user needs and preferences on the road.

In customer service applications, user preferences analysis can enhance the quality of interactions between AI systems and customers. By analyzing past interactions and feedback, developers can create systems that are more empathetic and responsive to customer needs. This can lead to higher customer satisfaction and loyalty, as well as improved overall customer experience.

In education, user preferences analysis can help in creating personalized learning experiences for students. By analyzing how students respond to different types of content (text, images, audio), developers can tailor educational materials to match individual learning styles. This can lead to better engagement, retention, and academic outcomes for students across various subjects and grade levels.

Chapter 7: Multimodal AI in Cybersecurity

Threat Detection and Response

Threat detection and response are crucial components of any AI system, especially in the increasingly complex and interconnected world of multimodal AI. With the ability to process and generate multiple types of data, AI systems are becoming more sophisticated in their capabilities, making them valuable assets in various industries.

In the realm of healthcare, multimodal AI systems play a vital role in assisting with diagnosis and treatment planning by analyzing medical images, text reports, and patient data. These systems can help healthcare professionals make more informed decisions, ultimately improving patient outcomes.

For autonomous vehicles, multimodal AI is essential for processing data from cameras, lidar, radar, and sensors to navigate and make real-time decisions. This technology is crucial for ensuring the safety and efficiency of self-driving cars, as it allows them to detect and respond to potential threats on the road.

In the realm of cybersecurity, multimodal AI systems are invaluable for detecting and responding to threats by analyzing text, network traffic, and system logs. These systems can help organizations stay ahead of potential cyber attacks and protect their sensitive data from being compromised.

Overall, the advancements in multimodal AI have opened up new possibilities for threat detection and response in various industries. By harnessing the power of AI systems that can process and generate multiple types of data, professionals can better protect their assets, make more informed decisions, and ultimately improve the efficiency and safety of their operations.

Text and Network Traffic Analysis

In the realm of AI systems that can process and generate multiple types of data, such as text, images, and audio, the field of multimodal AI is rapidly advancing. This expansion of capabilities has led to the development of more sophisticated virtual assistants and interactive AI systems that can understand and respond in more human-like ways. The ability to analyze and interpret various types of data simultaneously has opened up new possibilities for AI applications across a wide range of industries.

One of the key areas where multimodal AI is making a significant impact is in healthcare. AI systems that can analyze medical images, text reports, and patient data are being used to assist in diagnosis and treatment planning. By combining multiple types of data, these systems are able to provide more accurate and personalized recommendations, ultimately improving patient outcomes.

In the realm of autonomous vehicles, multimodal AI is playing a crucial role in enabling these vehicles to navigate and make decisions in real-time. By processing data from cameras, lidar, radar, and sensors simultaneously, AI systems can help autonomous vehicles safely navigate complex environments and avoid obstacles.

Customer service is another area where multimodal AI is revolutionizing the way businesses interact with their customers. AI systems that can analyze text, voice, and facial expressions are being used to provide personalized and empathetic responses to customers, enhancing the overall customer experience.

In education, multimodal AI is being used to adapt to different learning styles by incorporating text, images, and audio in interactive lessons and assessments. This personalized approach to learning is helping students of all ages and abilities to achieve better outcomes.

System Log Analysis

System log analysis is a crucial aspect of maintaining and optimizing Multimodal AI systems. By examining system logs, professionals can gain insights into the performance, efficiency, and security of their AI applications. These logs record important information such as user interactions, errors, warnings, resource usage, and system events, which can provide valuable data for troubleshooting and improvement.

One key benefit of system log analysis is the ability to identify and address issues in AI systems before they escalate. By monitoring system logs regularly, professionals can detect anomalies, errors, and performance bottlenecks that may impact the functionality and reliability of their AI applications. This proactive approach can help prevent system failures, minimize downtime, and optimize the overall performance of Multimodal AI systems.

In addition to troubleshooting, system log analysis can also be used for monitoring and optimizing the efficiency of AI applications. By analyzing system logs, professionals can gain insights into resource usage, response times, and system performance metrics, which can help in identifying areas for improvement and optimization. This data-driven approach can lead to more efficient and cost-effective Multimodal AI systems.

Furthermore, system log analysis plays a crucial role in ensuring the security and compliance of Multimodal AI applications. By monitoring system logs for suspicious activities, unauthorized access attempts, and security breaches, professionals can detect and respond to potential cybersecurity threats in a timely manner. This proactive approach can help in safeguarding sensitive data, protecting user privacy, and maintaining compliance with industry regulations.

Overall, system log analysis is an essential practice for professionals working with Multimodal AI systems. By leveraging the insights and data from system logs, professionals can enhance the performance, efficiency, security, and reliability of their AI applications. This proactive and data-driven approach can help in optimizing the functionality and effectiveness of Multimodal AI systems across various industries and use cases.

Chapter 8: Multimodal AI in Smart Homes

Voice Command Integration

Voice Command Integration is a key feature in the realm of Multimodal AI, allowing users to interact with AI systems using natural language commands. This integration has revolutionized the way we interact with technology, making it more intuitive and user-friendly. By simply speaking commands, users can control devices, access information, and perform tasks with ease, making the overall user experience more efficient and seamless.

In the field of healthcare, Voice Command Integration has proven to be invaluable, allowing medical professionals to access patient information and make critical decisions hands-free. By simply speaking commands, doctors can pull up medical records, analyze test results, and even dictate notes, saving valuable time and improving overall patient care. This technology has the potential to revolutionize the healthcare industry, making processes more streamlined and efficient.

Voice Command Integration is also playing a crucial role in the development of autonomous vehicles, allowing drivers to control their vehicles using voice commands. This technology not only enhances the overall driving experience but also improves safety by reducing distractions. By simply speaking commands, drivers can adjust settings, access navigation, and even make phone calls, all without taking their hands off the wheel. This technology has the potential to transform the way we interact with vehicles, making driving safer and more convenient.

In customer service, Voice Command Integration is being used to provide personalized and empathetic responses to customers. By analyzing voice commands, AI systems can understand customer needs and tailor responses accordingly, creating a more engaging and satisfying experience. This technology has the potential to revolutionize customer service, making interactions more efficient and effective, leading to increased customer satisfaction and loyalty.

Overall, Voice Command Integration is a game-changer in the world of Multimodal AI, allowing for more intuitive and natural interactions with technology. By simply speaking commands, users can control devices, access information, and perform tasks with ease, making the overall user experience more efficient and seamless. As this technology continues to evolve, we can expect to see even more advanced applications in various industries, further enhancing the capabilities of AI systems.

Sensor Data Automation

Sensor data automation plays a crucial role in the advancement of multimodal AI systems. By automating the collection, processing, and analysis of sensor data, AI systems can make faster and more accurate decisions in real-time. This is particularly important in applications such as autonomous vehicles, where sensors like cameras, lidar, radar, and GPS provide crucial information for navigation and obstacle avoidance.

In healthcare, sensor data automation can help AI systems analyze medical images, text reports, and patient data more efficiently. This can lead to faster and more accurate diagnosis and treatment planning, ultimately improving patient outcomes. By automating the process of collecting and analyzing sensor data, healthcare professionals can focus more on patient care and less on manual data processing.

In the realm of customer service, sensor data automation enables AI systems to analyze text, voice, and facial expressions to provide personalized and empathetic responses to customers. By automating the analysis of sensor data, AI systems can better understand customer needs and preferences, leading to more satisfying interactions and improved customer satisfaction.

In the field of education, sensor data automation allows AI systems to adapt to different learning styles by incorporating text, images, and audio in interactive lessons and assessments. This can help students learn more effectively and engage with the material in a more personalized way, ultimately leading to better educational outcomes. By automating the collection and analysis of sensor data, AI systems can provide more tailored and effective learning experiences for students.

Overall, sensor data automation is a critical component of multimodal AI systems across various industries, from healthcare to customer service to education. By automating the process of collecting, processing, and analyzing sensor data, AI systems can make faster and more accurate decisions, ultimately leading to improved outcomes for professionals and end-users alike.

Home Task Enhancement

In the world of Multimodal AI, the possibilities for enhancing home tasks are endless. Imagine a home where every appliance, every security measure, every task can be automated and optimized through the power of AI systems that can understand and respond to voice commands, images, and sensor data. From adjusting the temperature in your home to ensuring the security of your property, Multimodal AI for smart homes is revolutionizing the way we live.

One of the key benefits of incorporating Multimodal AI into our homes is the ability to automate repetitive tasks, saving time and energy for more important things. For example, AI systems can learn your daily routines and preferences, adjusting the lighting, temperature, and even the music in your home to create the perfect ambiance for any occasion. With the ability to understand and respond to voice commands, these systems can make life easier and more convenient for homeowners.

Enhancing security is another important aspect of Multimodal AI for smart homes. With the ability to analyze images and sensor data, AI systems can detect unusual activity or potential threats, alerting homeowners and taking necessary actions to ensure safety. Whether it's monitoring for intruders or detecting smoke or gas leaks, these systems provide peace of mind and security for homeowners.

Moreover, Multimodal AI for smart homes can also assist in managing energy consumption, optimizing resources, and reducing utility bills. By analyzing data from sensors and devices, AI systems can suggest ways to improve energy efficiency, reduce waste, and lower costs. From adjusting the thermostat based on occupancy to turning off lights in empty rooms, these systems are making homes more sustainable and environmentally friendly.

Overall, the integration of Multimodal AI into smart homes is transforming the way we live, making our lives easier, more secure, and more efficient. As technology continues to advance, the possibilities for enhancing home tasks through AI systems are limitless, offering a glimpse into a future where our homes are truly smart, responsive, and personalized to our needs.

Chapter 9: Multimodal AI in Finance

Investment Decision Making

Investment decision making is a crucial aspect of any business or individual looking to grow their wealth. With the advancements in multimodal AI, the process of making investment decisions has become more sophisticated and efficient. Multimodal AI systems can analyze a wide range of data sources, including text, images, audio, and more, to provide insights and recommendations for investment opportunities.

One of the key benefits of using multimodal AI for investment decision making is the ability to process vast amounts of data in real-time. Traditional investment analysis methods may be limited in scope and speed, but AI systems can quickly scan through news articles, financial reports, market data, and more to identify trends and patterns that may impact investment decisions. This real-time analysis can help investors stay ahead of the curve and make informed decisions based on the most up-to-date information available.

Multimodal AI can also help investors by providing personalized recommendations based on their individual preferences and risk tolerance. By analyzing text data from various sources, AI systems can tailor investment advice to suit each investor's unique goals and circumstances. This level of personalization can help investors make decisions that align with their long-term financial objectives and avoid unnecessary risks.

In addition to personalized recommendations, multimodal AI can also assist investors by providing insights into market sentiment and trends. By analyzing text data from social media platforms, news articles, and financial reports, AI systems can detect shifts in market sentiment and identify potential opportunities or risks. This information can help investors make more informed decisions and adapt their investment strategies accordingly.

Overall, the use of multimodal AI for investment decision making offers a wealth of benefits for professionals looking to enhance their investment strategies. By leveraging the power of AI systems that can process and generate multiple types of data, investors can gain valuable insights, personalized recommendations, and real-time analysis to make smarter and more profitable investment decisions.

News and Market Data Analysis

In the fast-paced world of artificial intelligence, the integration of multiple types of data has become increasingly important. Multimodal AI systems, which can process and generate various forms of data such as text, images, audio, and more, are revolutionizing the capabilities of AI applications. This advancement has paved the way for more sophisticated virtual assistants and interactive AI systems that can understand and respond in more human-like ways.

One of the key areas where multimodal AI is making a significant impact is in healthcare. AI systems that can analyze medical images, text reports, and patient data are being used to assist in diagnosis and treatment planning. These systems have the potential to revolutionize the healthcare industry by providing more accurate and efficient medical care.

Another area where multimodal AI is proving to be invaluable is in autonomous vehicles. AI systems that can process data from cameras, lidar, radar, and sensors are enabling vehicles to navigate and make decisions in real-time. This technology is critical for the development of self-driving cars and other autonomous vehicles that have the potential to revolutionize transportation.

In the realm of customer service, multimodal AI systems are being used to analyze text, voice, and facial expressions to provide personalized and empathetic responses to customers. This technology is revolutionizing the way businesses interact with their customers, providing a more personalized and efficient customer service experience.

Overall, the applications of multimodal AI are vast and varied, spanning industries such as education, media and entertainment, cybersecurity, finance, social media, language translation, and more. As these technologies continue to evolve, they have the potential to revolutionize the way we live and work, making our lives easier, more efficient, and more connected than ever before.

Financial Report Analysis

In the world of multimodal AI, the application of AI systems in various industries has revolutionized the way professionals approach data analysis and decision-making. One key area where multimodal AI is making a significant impact is in finance. With the ability to process and analyze text data from news articles and financial reports, as well as market data, AI systems are now being used to make investment decisions with greater accuracy and efficiency.

Financial report analysis is a crucial aspect of investment management, as it provides valuable insights into the financial health and performance of companies. By leveraging multimodal AI technologies, professionals in the finance industry can now extract key information from financial reports and news articles to make informed decisions about potential investments. These AI systems can analyze large volumes of data in real-time, allowing for faster and more accurate decision-making processes.

One of the main advantages of using multimodal AI for financial report analysis is the ability to detect trends and patterns that may not be immediately apparent to human analysts. By processing text data from a variety of sources, including news articles and financial reports, AI systems can identify key indicators of market trends and potential risks. This can help professionals in the finance industry to make more informed decisions about when to buy or sell investments, ultimately leading to better outcomes for their clients.

Furthermore, multimodal AI can also assist in predicting market movements based on the analysis of historical data and real-time market information. By combining text analysis with market data, AI systems can generate more accurate forecasts and recommendations for investment strategies. This can help professionals in the finance industry to stay ahead of market trends and make strategic decisions that maximize returns for their clients.

Overall, the use of multimodal AI for financial report analysis is transforming the way professionals in the finance industry approach investment management. By leveraging the power of AI systems to process and analyze diverse types of data, professionals can make more informed decisions, identify trends and patterns, and ultimately improve their investment strategies for better outcomes. As multimodal AI continues to advance, we can expect to see even greater innovations in financial report analysis that will further enhance the capabilities of professionals in the finance industry.

Chapter 10: Multimodal AI in Social Media

Trend Detection

Trend detection is a crucial aspect of Multimodal AI, as it allows professionals to stay ahead of the curve in various industries. With the ability to process and generate multiple types of data, AI systems can now analyze trends in text, images, audio, and more to provide valuable insights for decision-making. This expanded capability has revolutionized the way businesses operate, as they can now leverage AI to predict market trends, customer preferences, and emerging technologies.

In the healthcare sector, Multimodal AI is being used to detect trends in medical data to assist in diagnosis and treatment planning. By analyzing medical images, text reports, and patient data, AI systems can identify patterns and anomalies that may not be apparent to human professionals. This has the potential to revolutionize healthcare by improving accuracy, efficiency, and patient outcomes.

Similarly, in the field of autonomous vehicles, Multimodal AI is essential for trend detection in real-time data from cameras, lidar, radar, and sensors. This allows AI systems to navigate complex environments, make split-second decisions, and adapt to changing road conditions. By detecting trends in traffic patterns, pedestrian behavior, and weather conditions, autonomous vehicles can operate safely and efficiently on the road.

In customer service, Multimodal AI is used to detect trends in text, voice, and facial expressions to provide personalized and empathetic responses to customers. By analyzing customer interactions across multiple channels, AI systems can identify trends in customer satisfaction, preferences, and sentiment. This enables businesses to improve customer service, build stronger relationships, and increase loyalty.

Overall, trend detection in Multimodal AI is a powerful tool for professionals across various industries. By leveraging AI systems that can process and generate multiple types of data, professionals can stay ahead of the curve, make informed decisions, and drive innovation in their respective fields. As technology continues to advance, the capabilities of Multimodal AI for trend detection will only continue to grow, reshaping the way we work, live, and interact with the world around us.

Sentiment Analysis

In the realm of multimodal AI, one of the key areas of focus is sentiment analysis. Sentiment analysis involves the use of AI algorithms to determine the emotional tone behind a piece of text, speech, or image. This capability allows AI systems to understand and respond to human emotions, making them more intuitive and empathetic in their interactions with users. Sentiment analysis is particularly important in applications like virtual assistants, customer service, and social media, where understanding and responding to emotions can greatly enhance the user experience.

In healthcare, sentiment analysis can be used to assess patient feedback and improve the quality of care. By analyzing text reports, patient data, and even facial expressions, AI systems can better understand the emotional state of patients and tailor their responses accordingly. This can lead to more personalized and effective treatment plans, ultimately improving patient outcomes.

In autonomous vehicles, sentiment analysis can be crucial for ensuring the safety and comfort of passengers. By analyzing data from cameras, lidar, radar, and sensors, AI systems can detect signs of distress or discomfort in passengers and adjust the vehicle's behavior accordingly. This can help create a more pleasant and secure driving experience, particularly in challenging or high-stress situations.

In the realm of customer service, sentiment analysis can help AI systems provide more empathetic and personalized responses to customers. By analyzing text, voice, and facial expressions, AI systems can gauge the emotional state of customers and tailor their responses to meet their needs. This can lead to improved customer satisfaction and loyalty, ultimately benefiting the business.

Overall, sentiment analysis plays a crucial role in enhancing the capabilities of multimodal AI systems across a wide range of applications. By enabling AI systems to understand and respond to human emotions, sentiment analysis helps create more intuitive, empathetic, and effective AI solutions for professionals in various industries.

Fake News Detection

Fake news has become a pervasive issue in today's digital age, with misinformation spreading rapidly across various platforms. In response to this challenge, researchers and developers have been working on developing advanced AI systems capable of detecting and combating fake news. These systems leverage multimodal AI technology, which enables them to process and analyze multiple types of data, including text, images, and audio, to identify misleading or false information.

One of the key advantages of using multimodal AI for fake news detection is its ability to cross-reference information from different sources and modalities. By analyzing text content alongside images or audio, AI systems can better assess the credibility and accuracy of news articles or social media posts. This multimodal approach helps to uncover inconsistencies or discrepancies that may indicate the presence of fake news, allowing for more effective detection and filtering of misinformation.

In the realm of social media, where fake news can quickly go viral and influence public opinion, multimodal AI systems play a crucial role in monitoring and flagging suspicious content. By analyzing text, images, and audio from posts and comments, these systems can identify patterns and trends associated with fake news dissemination. This proactive approach helps to limit the spread of misinformation and protect users from being misled by false or misleading information.

Moreover, multimodal AI can also be used to evaluate the reliability of news sources and websites by analyzing a combination of textual information, visual cues, and metadata. By assessing the credibility of sources based on multiple modalities, AI systems can provide users with more accurate and trustworthy information. This not only helps individuals make more informed decisions but also contributes to building a more transparent and trustworthy digital ecosystem.

Overall, the integration of multimodal AI technology into fake news detection represents a significant step towards combating misinformation and promoting digital literacy. By harnessing the power of AI to analyze diverse types of data, including text, images, and audio, we can enhance our ability to discern between fact and fiction in an increasingly complex media landscape. As professionals in the field of AI, it is essential to continue advancing these capabilities to ensure the integrity and reliability of information in the digital age.

Chapter 11: Multimodal AI in Language Translation

Real-time Translation

Real-time translation is a cutting-edge application of multimodal AI that is revolutionizing the way we communicate in a globalized world. Gone are the days of struggling to understand foreign languages or relying on clunky translation devices – with real-time translation technology, language barriers are becoming a thing of the past.

One of the key benefits of real-time translation is its ability to facilitate seamless communication across different languages and cultures. Whether you're traveling abroad, conducting business with international partners, or simply trying to connect with someone who speaks a different language, real-time translation can help bridge the gap and ensure that everyone is on the same page.

In the realm of healthcare, real-time translation is particularly valuable for assisting medical professionals in communicating with patients who speak different languages. By enabling real-time translation of medical reports, patient data, and even live conversations, healthcare providers can ensure that every patient receives the care and attention they need, regardless of language barriers.

In the field of customer service, real-time translation is also proving to be a game-changer. AI systems that can analyze text, voice, and facial expressions can provide personalized and empathetic responses to customers, enhancing the overall customer experience and building stronger relationships with clients from diverse backgrounds.

Overall, real-time translation is a powerful tool that is transforming the way we communicate and interact with others in an increasingly interconnected world. As multimodal AI continues to advance, we can expect real-time translation technology to become even more sophisticated and widely used in a variety of industries and applications.

Communication Facilitation

Communication facilitation is a key aspect of advancing multimodal AI systems, as they are designed to process and generate multiple types of data such as text, images, and audio. These systems are becoming more prevalent in various industries, expanding the capabilities of AI applications to interact with users in more sophisticated and human-like ways. This has led to the development of virtual assistants and interactive AI systems that can understand and respond to users in a more personalized manner.

In the field of healthcare, multimodal AI systems play a crucial role in assisting medical professionals with diagnosis and treatment planning. These systems can analyze medical images, text reports, and patient data to provide valuable insights and recommendations. By incorporating multiple types of data, healthcare professionals can make more informed decisions and improve patient outcomes.

Multimodal AI is also revolutionizing the way autonomous vehicles navigate and make decisions in real-time. These systems can process data from cameras, lidar, radar, and sensors to ensure safe and efficient driving. By combining different types of data, autonomous vehicles can better understand their surroundings and respond to changing road conditions, ultimately enhancing road safety for passengers and pedestrians.

In customer service, multimodal AI systems are being used to analyze text, voice, and facial expressions to provide personalized and empathetic responses to customers. By incorporating multiple modalities, these systems can better understand customer needs and preferences, leading to improved customer satisfaction and loyalty. This personalized approach to customer service is revolutionizing the way businesses interact with their customers.

Overall, communication facilitation is a critical component of advancing multimodal AI systems across various industries. By incorporating multiple types of data, these systems can understand

and respond to users in more human-like ways, leading to more personalized and efficient interactions. From healthcare to autonomous vehicles to customer service, multimodal AI is transforming the way we communicate and interact with technology in our daily lives.

Text, Speech, and Image Translation

In the realm of multimodal AI, the ability to translate between text, speech, and images is a crucial component that has revolutionized the way we interact with technology. Gone are the days of relying solely on text-based inputs and outputs; now, AI systems can seamlessly process and generate information in multiple formats, opening up a world of possibilities for more intuitive and human-like interactions.

Text, speech, and image translation capabilities have paved the way for the development of more sophisticated virtual assistants and interactive AI systems. By being able to understand and respond to a variety of data types, these systems can provide more personalized and empathetic responses, making interactions with technology feel more natural and intuitive for users.

In the healthcare industry, multimodal AI systems are being utilized to analyze medical images, text reports, and patient data for more accurate diagnosis and treatment planning. By combining information from different sources, these systems can provide healthcare professionals with a more comprehensive understanding of a patient's condition, leading to better outcomes and more personalized care.

In the realm of autonomous vehicles, text, speech, and image translation capabilities are essential for processing data from cameras, lidar, radar, and sensors to navigate and make decisions in real-time. By being able to interpret and respond to a variety of inputs, AI systems in autonomous vehicles can operate more safely and efficiently, helping to usher in the era of self-driving cars.

Overall, the ability to translate between text, speech, and images is a game-changer in the world of multimodal AI, opening up new possibilities for more sophisticated and intuitive interactions with technology across a wide range of industries and applications. As these capabilities continue to advance, we can expect to see even more innovative and transformative uses of AI in the future.

Chapter 12: Conclusion

Summary of Key Points

Summary of Key Points:

1. Multimodal AI systems are becoming increasingly prevalent in various industries, allowing for more sophisticated applications that can process and generate multiple types of data such as text, images, and audio. This has expanded the capabilities of AI, enabling more human-like interactions with virtual assistants and interactive systems.

2. In the healthcare sector, Multimodal AI is being used to analyze medical images, text reports, and patient data to assist in diagnosis and treatment planning. This technology is revolutionizing the way medical professionals make decisions and provide care to patients.

3. Autonomous vehicles are benefiting from Multimodal AI systems that can process data from cameras, lidar, radar, and sensors to navigate and make real-time decisions. This technology is crucial for the development of safe and efficient self-driving cars.

4. Customer service is being enhanced by Multimodal AI systems that can analyze text, voice, and facial expressions to provide personalized and empathetic responses to customers. This helps companies improve customer satisfaction and loyalty.

5. Multimodal AI is also being utilized in education, media and entertainment, cybersecurity, smart homes, finance, social media, and language translation. These applications are transforming the way we interact with technology and are paving the way for a more connected and intelligent future.

Future Trends in Multimodal AI

The field of multimodal AI is rapidly evolving, with new trends emerging that are shaping the future of AI applications across various industries. From virtual assistants to autonomous vehicles, the capabilities of multimodal AI systems are expanding, allowing for more sophisticated and human-like interactions. These advancements are enabling AI systems to process and generate multiple types of data, including text, images, and audio, leading to more personalized and empathetic responses in a wide range of applications.

One of the key trends in multimodal AI is its application in healthcare. AI systems are now able to analyze medical images, text reports, and patient data to assist in diagnosis and treatment planning. This has the potential to revolutionize healthcare by improving the accuracy and efficiency of medical decisions, ultimately leading to better patient outcomes. Additionally, multimodal AI is being used in autonomous vehicles to process data from cameras, lidar, radar, and sensors to navigate and make decisions in real-time. This technology is paving the way for safer and more efficient transportation systems.

In the realm of customer service, multimodal AI systems are being developed to analyze text, voice, and facial expressions to provide personalized and empathetic responses to customers. This level of customization and understanding is enhancing the customer experience and improving overall satisfaction. In education, multimodal AI systems are adapting to different learning styles by incorporating text, images, and audio in interactive lessons and assessments. This personalized approach to education is revolutionizing the way students learn and engage with course material.

In media and entertainment, multimodal AI systems are generating personalized recommendations and content based on user preferences across different types of media. This level of personalization is enhancing the user experience and driving greater engagement with content. In cybersecurity, multimodal AI systems are detecting and responding to threats by analyzing text, network traffic, and system logs. This proactive approach to cybersecurity is essential in protecting sensitive data and preventing cyber attacks. Overall, the future trends in multimodal AI are shaping a world where AI systems can process and generate multiple types of data in more sophisticated and human-like ways, leading to a wide range of applications that are revolutionizing industries and enhancing everyday experiences.

Recommendations for Professionals

In order to effectively utilize multimodal AI in various industries, professionals must consider several key recommendations. Firstly, it is crucial for professionals to stay updated on the latest advancements in multimodal AI technology. This includes attending conferences, workshops, and online courses to enhance their knowledge and skills in this rapidly evolving field. By staying informed, professionals can adapt to new trends and techniques, ultimately improving the performance of AI systems in their respective industries.

Secondly, professionals should collaborate with experts from different disciplines to leverage their expertise and insights in multimodal AI applications. For example, in healthcare, professionals can work with radiologists, data scientists, and healthcare providers to develop AI systems that can accurately analyze medical images, text reports, and patient data for improved diagnosis and treatment planning. By fostering interdisciplinary collaborations, professionals can harness the full potential of multimodal AI technology for innovative solutions in their fields.

Furthermore, professionals should prioritize data quality and diversity when training multimodal AI systems. It is essential to collect diverse and high-quality datasets that represent the variability and complexity of real-world scenarios. This ensures that AI systems can generalize well and perform effectively across different modalities, such as text, images, audio, and video. By focusing on data quality and diversity, professionals can enhance the accuracy, reliability, and robustness of multimodal AI applications in various domains.

Another important recommendation for professionals is to prioritize ethical considerations when developing and deploying multimodal AI systems. This includes ensuring transparency, fairness, accountability, and privacy in AI algorithms and decision-making processes. Professionals should adhere to ethical guidelines and regulations to prevent biases, discrimination, and misuse of AI technologies. By promoting ethical practices, professionals can build trust with stakeholders and users, ultimately fostering the responsible and sustainable development of multimodal AI solutions.

Lastly, professionals should continuously evaluate and optimize multimodal AI systems to improve their performance, efficiency, and user experience. This involves conducting thorough experiments, tests, and validations to identify strengths and weaknesses in AI models and algorithms. By iteratively refining and fine-tuning AI systems, professionals can enhance their capabilities and address any challenges or limitations in multimodal AI applications. Overall, by following these recommendations, professionals can harness the power of multimodal AI technology to drive innovation, transformation, and impact in their respective industries.

www.ingramcontent.com/pod-product-compliance
Lightning Source LLC
Chambersburg PA
CBHW080435240526
45479CB00016B/1305